Ria and Vik's Seasonal Adventures

Written By: Neeti Agarwal

Illustrated By: Nia Kurniaawati

We think outside the box.

To request permissions, contact the publisher at RiaandVik@tobschool.com

ISBN : 979-8-9884992-0-6 (Paperback)
ISBN : 979-8-9884992-1-3 (Ebook)

First paperback edition June 2023

Any references to historical events, real people, or real places are used fictiously. Names, characters, and places are products of the author's imagination.

Published by :
TOBschool
1643 Valle Verde Drive
Brentwood TN, 37027

www.tobschool.com

Dedicated to Shishir and Riya.
You are the wind beneath my wings.

Thank you to Rishaan for being the first reader.

Ria and Vik are best friends who love exploring and learning new things. Ria is a curious and creative girl who loves exploring the outdoors, and Vik is her adventurous best friend who is always up for a new challenge.

One day while playing outside, they noticed the sun shining brightly and the air felt warmer on their skin. They remembered how cold and rainy it had been the day before. So they decided to ask their teacher, Mrs. Johnson, why the weather had changed.

"Ah, the weather has changed because the season has shifted from winter to spring," Mrs. Johnson explained. Ria and Vik became curious and asked if there were other seasons.

"Absolutely! There are four seasons— spring, summer, fall, and winter— and each one is special in its own way," Mrs. Johnson replied.

Mrs. Johnson explained how the seasons bring about changes in weather, nature, and the activities we do.

"In the spring, trees grow leaves, and flowers bloom. Birds begin to fly and sing. In the summer, we visit the beach to enjoy the blue sea and sand. We eat ice cream to stay cool."

"Then, in the fall, the leaves on trees change color and fall off. We enjoy jumping into the leaves and having a great time. In the winter, we make snowmen when we see snow falling from the sky. We also have hot cocoa to keep us warm," she added.

Ria and Vik's eyes widened with wonder as they listened to Mrs. Johnson's explanation. They had never thought about the seasons in that way before, and it made them excited to learn more.

Seeing the excitement in Ria and Vik, Mrs. Johnson decided to do a fun project with them. She gave them four clear jars, a jug of water, and blue, red, green, and yellow food coloring.

"We will be using these items to learn about how temperature affects the jars," Mrs. Johnson said.

 Mrs. Johnson asked Ria and Vik to carefully fill each jar with water and add a different color of food coloring to each one. Ria filled the four jars with water, and Vik added blue color in the jar labeled "Jar 1", red color in "Jar 2", green color in "Jar 3", and yellow color in "Jar 4."

Mrs. Johnson then placed the blue jar in the freezer, the red jar in the refrigerator, the green jar on the lunch table in the classroom, and the yellow jar outside in the play area where there was sun.

"I can't wait to see what happens to our jars!" Ria said, tapping her foot impatiently. "I think the blue jar will turn into ice," said Vik, remembering how water had turned into ice when his mother had put it in the freezer. "But I'm excited to see what happens to the other jars," he added.

As time went by, they kept checking on their jars, and they noticed some interesting changes! The water in the blue jar had transformed into a beautiful shade of blue ice, just like magic! The red jar had become cooler, but not frozen, and the green jar felt the same, but the yellow jar felt warmer than the others.

Ria and Vik couldn't contain their excitement and immediately started drawing pictures of each jar and the changes they observed. As they drew, they chatted about their observations and brainstormed fun ways to use the jars to showcase the different seasons.

"The blue jar feels like winter because it's frozen and cold," Ria said.

"And the yellow jar feels like summer because it's warm and sunny!" Vik added.

They told their teacher, Mrs. Johnson, that the blue jar feels like winter, the red jar feels like fall, the green jar feels like spring, and the yellow jar feels like summer.

"Amazing, Ria and Vik! I am proud of you both," Mrs. Johnson exclaimed.

Ria and Vik were thrilled to hear this. They decided to start a nature journal where they would document their observations when seasons change. Their exploration of the seasons with their teacher taught them that nature is full of wonders and surprises and that there's always something new to learn and discover if we keep an open and curious mind.

About the Author

Neeti Agarwal has a great passion for activity-based learning. She believes that children learn best when they are engaged in fun and interactive activities that help them explore and discover new things.

Neeti is an engineer and has always been fascinated by the way things work. She loves to tinker with gadgets and figure out how they function. This love for problem-solving has inspired her to create stories that not only entertain but also teach children about science and math.

Neeti currently lives in Brentwood, Tennessee, with her husband and daughter, where she enjoys spending time with her family.

Made in the USA
Columbia, SC
17 June 2023